17046

j612   Zim, Herbert S.
ZIM
        Blood

17046

© THE BAKER & TAYLOR CO

17646

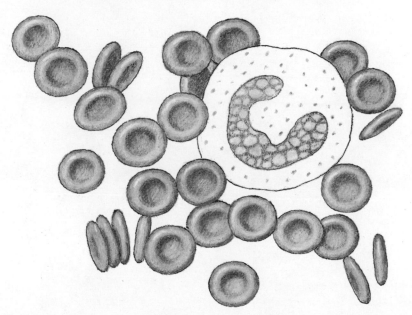

BLOOD

HERBERT S. ZIM

illustrated by RENÉ MARTIN

William Morrow & Company   New York

    7 8 9

The author wishes to thank Roger K. Haugen, M.D., Pathologist,
Holy Cross Hospital, Fort Lauderdale, Florida, for checking text and
art. Also, James R. Skelly, for his research assistance.

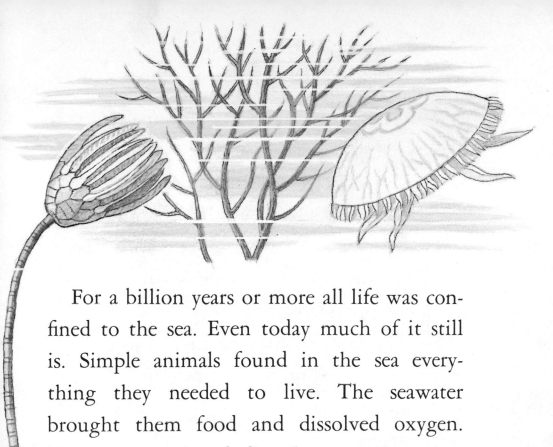

For a billion years or more all life was confined to the sea. Even today much of it still
is. Simple animals found in the sea every-
thing they needed to live. The seawater
brought them food and dissolved oxygen.
Their wastes passed directly into the ocean,
since most of the cells of the animal's body
were in contact with the seawater.

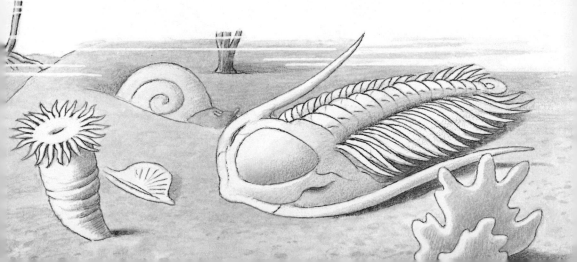

Animals began to move to land less than half a billion years ago. Their bodies changed. Even new organs formed, enabling them to live on dry land and in the open air. But every cell of every animal's body still needed the moisture, food, and oxygen that the sea had once provided.

Cells in contact with the air had to be protected from drying out. Many land animals

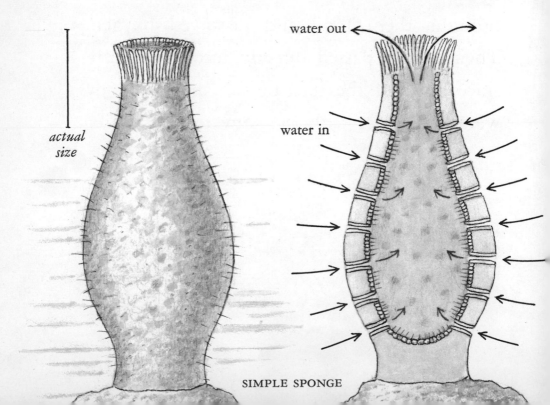

actual size

water out

water in

SIMPLE SPONGE

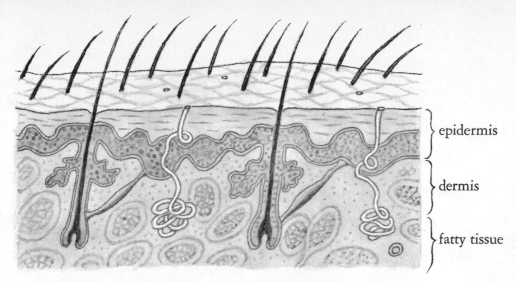

epidermis

dermis

fatty tissue

A COMPLEX PROTECTIVE SKIN HELPS MAMMALS LIVE ON LAND.

developed a tough skin as a protective en-
velope. An improved skeleton gave land animals support, and stronger muscles made rapid
movement on land possible. Slow crawlers
gave way to animals that walked and ran.

With better sense organs, animals became
more aware of their surroundings. They could
see, hear, feel, taste, and smell better than
most sea animals. Thus they could find food
and avoid enemies better.

The tissues of the animal's body that changed with life on land are what we sometimes call "solid flesh." All that is, except for one, the blood. Blood is a liquid that still does for your body what the ocean did for tiny marine creatures long ago.

Blood is the liquid tissue that brings food and oxygen to each body cell. Then it takes away the wastes. It does more—so much more, that blood has become one of the most complicated tissues of the body. Only the brain itself is more intricate.

Many living cells and much non-living material are in the blood, in which hundreds if not thousands of chemicals are dissolved. Some of these materials are so potent that a barely visible amount can make the difference between life and death.

You might think that because blood is a liquid it contains a great deal of water. Actually blood contains only a little more water than other soft parts of your body. The tissues of your liver are made up of about 70 percent water. Muscles have about 75 percent water in them. Your kidneys and brain contain about 80 percent water, and so does your blood.

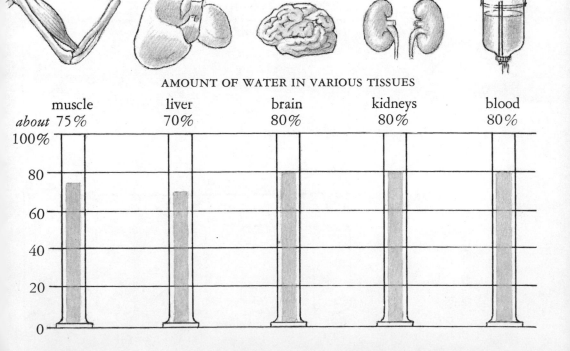

AMOUNT OF WATER IN VARIOUS TISSUES

	muscle	liver	brain	kidneys	blood
about	75%	70%	80%	80%	80%

A grown person loses about two and a half quarts of water daily. To keep the body in balance, this amount or more must be obtained from food and drink. Soon after water enters the body, it enters the blood. With a number of chemicals dissolved in it, this water moves from the blood into the tissues and out again many times during the day. It bathes most of the body cells and acts as a messenger between them and the outside world.

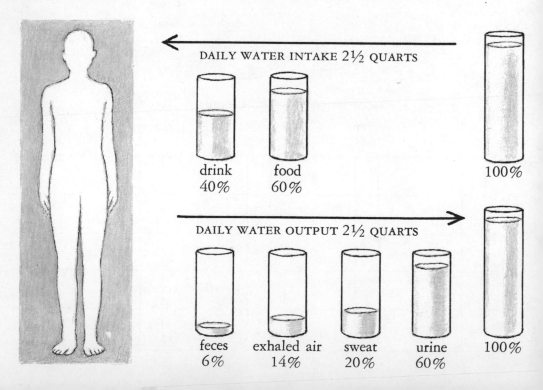

DAILY WATER INTAKE 2½ QUARTS

drink 40%   food 60%   100%

DAILY WATER OUTPUT 2½ QUARTS

feces 6%   exhaled air 14%   sweat 20%   urine 60%   100%

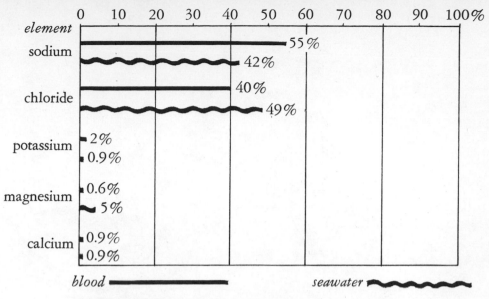

PERCENTAGE OF SOLIDS IN BLOOD AND SEAWATER

The sea is not pure water. Many chemicals are dissolved in it, making up about three percent of seawater. The most common is ordinary table salt. Blood also contains salt, and many more chemicals. Take out the living cells, and what is left of the blood is a liquid, the blood plasma. Plasma is 90 to 92 percent water, compared to the sea, which is 97 percent water. Your blood contains two to three times as much chemical material as does the sea.

WITH FOOD BUT NO WATER
A MAN CAN LIVE ABOUT 4 DAYS.

WITH WATER BUT NO FOOD
A MAN CAN LIVE ABOUT 90 DAYS.

If your body loses too much water, the blood thickens and acts as a signal for your protection. The kidneys slow down in making urine. In your throat you recognize the feeling you call thirst. Soon after you have drunk, water enters the blood until it becomes a better balanced mixture of water, chemicals, and cells.

About 45 percent of your blood—nearly half—is the living cells. The rest is the clear, light yellow liquid, plasma.

If a test tube of blood is allowed to stand and clot, the cells and some of the chemicals settle out. The liquid that separates from the blood clot is blood serum. It is almost the same as plasma, but does not contain the chemicals that aid clotting.

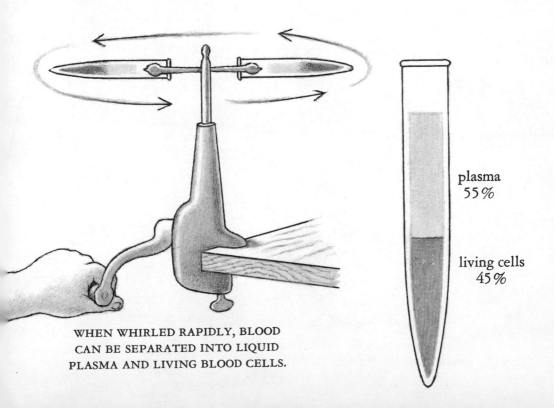

plasma 55%

living cells 45%

WHEN WHIRLED RAPIDLY, BLOOD CAN BE SEPARATED INTO LIQUID PLASMA AND LIVING BLOOD CELLS.

The best known part of the blood consists of the red cells. If you've ever cut your finger, you have seen these cells by the millions. But to see each single red cell, which doctors call an erythrocyte, requires a medical microscope. Each red blood cell has the same general shape as that of a coin, but the ridge around the edge is higher and wider than you find on a dime or a penny.

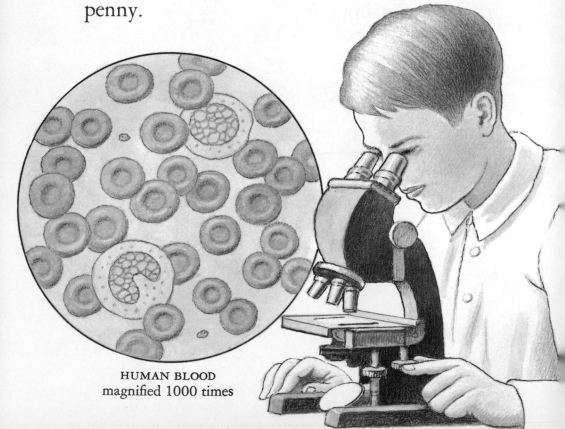

HUMAN BLOOD
magnified 1000 times

Red blood cells have been carefully measured. They average a bit more than seven microns wide and two microns thick. A micron is only about one twenty-five-thousandth of an inch, so if red blood cells were put one on top of the other, like a pile of dimes, 12 thousand or so would make a pile one inch high.

Every red blood cell is alive. It uses food and oxygen. But it is a special kind of cell. It does not contain a nucleus like most other cells, and so it cannot divide and reproduce. Instead, red blood cells are manufactured in the soft marrow of your bones. Before birth some of the red cells are also manufactured in the spleen and liver. However, it is the marrow of bones that makes most of the red blood cells. The marrow in arms and

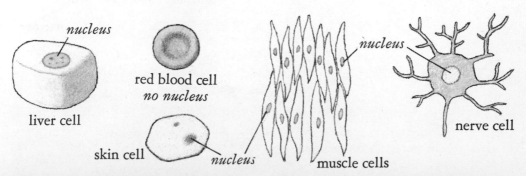

MOST BODY CELLS HAVE A NUCLEUS, BUT NOT RED BLOOD CELLS.

legs is most productive in children. The marrow in the spine and ribs supplies the most for grown-ups.

Your bones produce about one half a cup of red blood cells daily. This amount is about enough to replace those that are aged, damaged, or abnormal. On an average, red blood cells live for 100 to 120 days. They are destroyed by large cells in the spleen when they become old or injured.

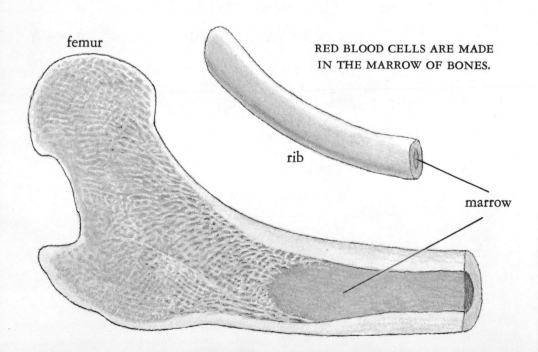

femur

rib

RED BLOOD CELLS ARE MADE IN THE MARROW OF BONES.

marrow

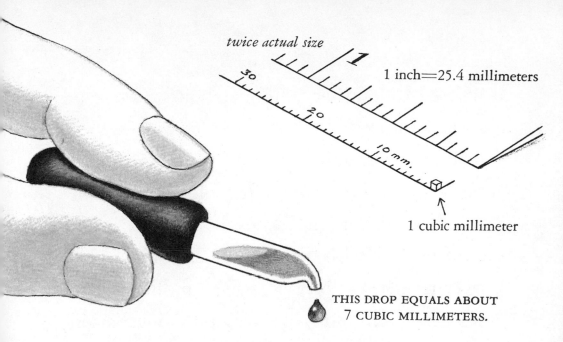

twice actual size

30

20

10 mm.

1

1 inch=25.4 millimeters

1 cubic millimeter

THIS DROP EQUALS ABOUT
7 CUBIC MILLIMETERS.

As a result, there is a balance between red blood cells produced and red blood cells destroyed. About one percent, or a little less, of your red blood cells is replaced daily. This small percentage, however, amounts to 250 or 300 billion red blood cells. A grown person has about 35 trillion red blood cells moving around his body. To simplify the problem of counting them, doctors usually report the number of red blood cells in one cubic millimeter of blood—an amount about the size of a small drop.

Each cubic millimeter of your blood contains about five million red blood cells. The number will vary in sickness or in health, with climate and with altitude. It also differs between men (closer to five million) and women (four and a half million). A variation of ten percent, more or less, is normal.

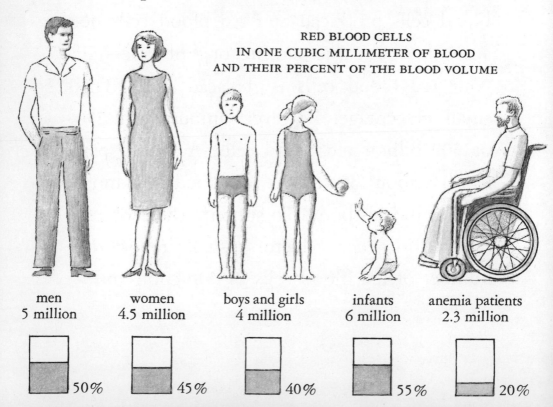

RED BLOOD CELLS
IN ONE CUBIC MILLIMETER OF BLOOD
AND THEIR PERCENT OF THE BLOOD VOLUME

men 5 million	women 4.5 million	boys and girls 4 million	infants 6 million	anemia patients 2.3 million
50%	45%	40%	55%	20%

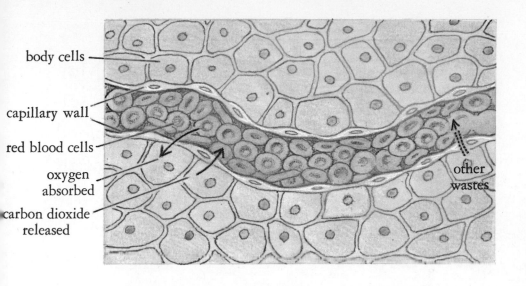

body cells

capillary wall

red blood cells

oxygen absorbed

carbon dioxide released

other wastes

The work of red blood cells is mainly to aid respiration, the process by which living cells absorb oxygen and release carbon-dioxide gas. Respiration makes it possible for cells to oxidize food and thus grow. In your lungs, oxygen is absorbed on the surface of red blood cells. Later it is released in the tissues. The total surface of the red cells in your body that transport oxygen adds up to about 3000 square yards—over half an acre.

In the ocean, the living cells of a jellyfish only get the oxygen that is dissolved in seawater. Oxygen is also dissolved in your blood plasma, but not nearly enough for the needs of your body. Most of the oxygen your body uses is transported by red blood cells, which hold the oxygen in a loose chemical combination. Red cells deliver about 60 times more oxygen than your blood plasma alone could supply.

Your need for oxygen changes with rest, work, and play. During sleep you breathe in about 8 quarts of air a minute. When you are active, you need more. To supply more oxygen to muscles and other cells, you breathe faster. After a hard race, you may take in as much as 400 quarts of air a minute.

sleeping

15	BREATHS
65	HEARTBEATS
	(*per minute*)

At the same time your heart beats faster and pumps more blood. At rest, it pumps about 6 quarts a minute; during heavy activity, it pumps as much as 17 quarts.

Not only does your blood circulate faster, more is made available to carry oxygen. Your spleen stores red blood cells. As much as 20 percent of your blood cells may accumulate there. With activity or excitement, the spleen releases extra blood cells to carry more oxygen to the other body cells.

standing	walking	running	chopping	
15	22	45	45	BREATHS
86	105	180	200	HEARTBEATS
				(per minute)

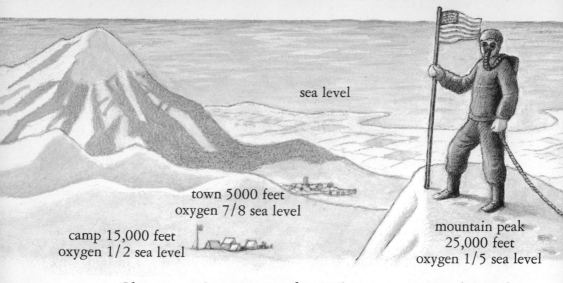

sea level

town 5000 feet
oxygen 7/8 sea level

camp 15,000 feet
oxygen 1/2 sea level

mountain peak
25,000 feet
oxygen 1/5 sea level

Slower changes take place in the blood when a person moves from sea level to mountaintops, where there is less oxygen because there is less air. Each breath yields less oxygen, and so the body forms more red blood cells to extract as much oxygen as possible from the thin air. At high places people have a higher red blood count. In the Andes mountains, Indians may have a blood count of eight million red cells per cubic millimeter.

The material in red blood cells that transports oxygen is a complex chemical called hemoglobin. This red chemical is related to chlorophyll—the green chemical that enables plants to manufacture food.

Hemoglobin forms a chemical combination with oxygen. When conditions change slightly, the oxygen is released. Thus the red cells pick up oxygen in the lungs, carry it to the body cells, where it is released and used. At any moment about one quart of oxygen is being carried by your blood. This amount is only enough to meet your body's needs for a few minutes, even when you are not active. If cells, especially brain cells, lack oxygen for a few minutes they can be seriously injured.

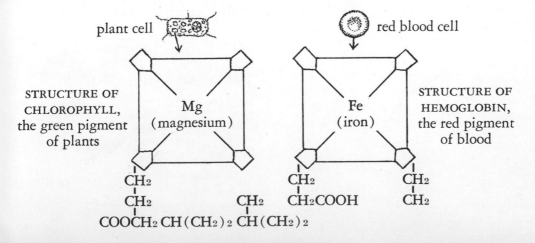

plant cell

red blood cell

STRUCTURE OF CHLOROPHYLL, the green pigment of plants

Mg (magnesium)

Fe (iron)

STRUCTURE OF HEMOGLOBIN, the red pigment of blood

CH_2
CH_2
$COOCH_2$ $CH(CH_2)_2$ $CH(CH_2)_2$

CH_2
CH_2COOH

CH_2
CH_2

ARTERIAL PRESSURE POINTS
TO STOP BLEEDING
Press between the wound and
the heart at one of these points.

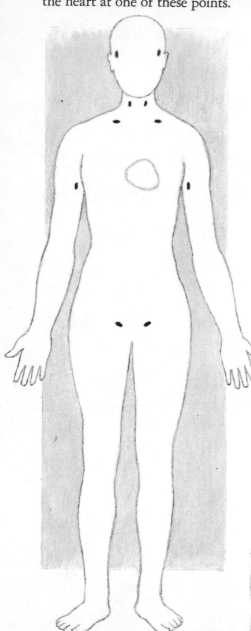

Because red blood cells are so important, anything that happens to them—such as a disease that reduces their number, or their ability to carry oxygen—is serious. The poison of rattlesnakes, scorpions, and centipedes destroys red blood cells. So does the tiny malaria parasite which still is common in warmer parts of the world.

 FIRST AID RULES
WITH SEVERE BLEEDING
1 Stop bleeding.
2 Treat shock.
3 Get help.

A large wound or injury may also cause a severe loss of red blood cells. Immediately the body takes steps to keep down the loss and to release the blood stored in the spleen.

The loss of a pint of blood, as much as a man gives when he donates to a blood bank, does not have much effect on the body. However, the bone marrow needs from six to eight weeks to make enough red blood cells to bring the blood back to normal. The loss of a quart of blood has more serious effects. If two quarts are lost, the results can be fatal unless the blood is replaced immediately.

Luckily, blood can be replaced by transfusion. This process once meant letting blood

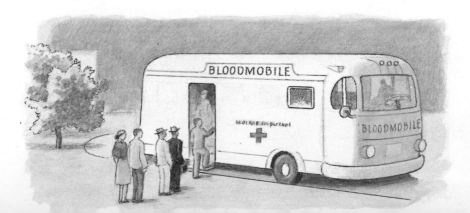

from one person flow directly into the vein of a sick or injured person. Nowadays blood is stored and kept on hand for an emergency. Transfusions have saved thousands of lives, not only of injured people, but of people who have had major operations or blood diseases.

Blood transfusions require care, because all blood is not the same. Human blood falls into four great groups. The classification depends on whether key protein chemicals are present in the red cells and the blood serum.

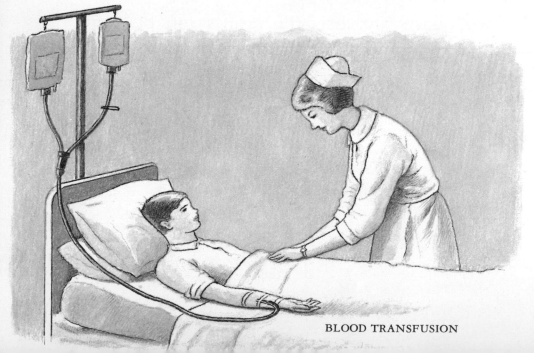

BLOOD TRANSFUSION

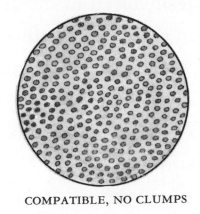
COMPATIBLE, NO CLUMPS

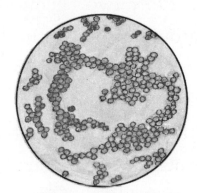
INCOMPATIBLE, CLUMPS

When red cells from one blood group are mixed with serum from another blood group, the red blood cells may clump. This effect is due to the action of chemicals, called antibodies, formed in the blood plasma. Your blood builds these antibodies as a protection against foreign proteins, such as those of a virus or bacteria. If blood of the wrong type is used in a transfusion, this protective action may form clumps of red cells that may block vital organs.

Only two chemicals are involved in blood grouping. One forms blood group A; the other forms blood group B. When neither is present, the blood is put in group O. When both chemicals are present, the blood is put in group AB. Thus there are four blood groups.

The plasma of any blood will not, of course, clump red cells of the same blood group. But the plasma of a patient getting a transfusion may clump the cells from another blood group. This

TYPICAL REACTIONS IN MIXING BLOOD

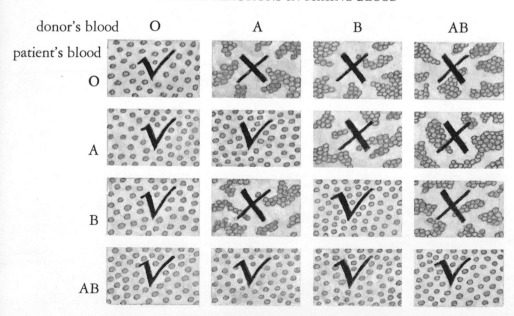

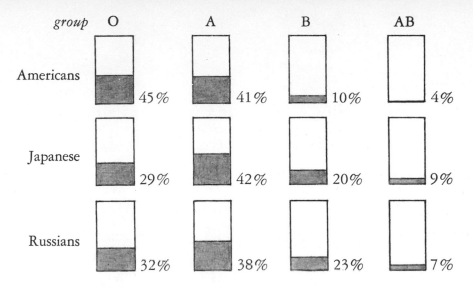

group	O	A	B	AB
Americans	45%	41%	10%	4%
Japanese	29%	42%	20%	9%
Russians	32%	38%	23%	7%

THE NUMBER OF PEOPLE IN EACH BLOOD GROUP VARIES.

is shown in the table above. A person with AB blood has both A and B chemicals in it, and so he can receive all types of blood. A person with type O blood lacks both A and B chemicals, and so he can receive only type O blood in a transfusion. But since type O blood lacks both A and B factors, people with any type blood can accept it.

BLOOD BAG LABELS SHOW BLOOD GROUP AND RH TYPE.

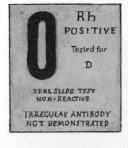
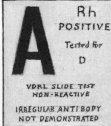
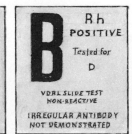
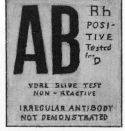

One other of the many blood antibodies may sometimes cause trouble. It is the Rh blood factor, so called because it was first discovered in the rhesus monkey. Most of the people (about 85 percent in the United States) have blood that is Rh positive. A few have inherited the condition that makes their blood Rh negative.

If a person with Rh negative blood needs a blood transfusion, he should receive Rh negative blood—of the proper blood group, of course. If the Rh negative person receives Rh positive blood, nothing seems to happen. But his Rh negative blood builds up antibodies against the Rh positive blood. If he gets more transfusions of Rh positive blood, the antibodies formed in his own blood will destroy the red blood cells he receives.

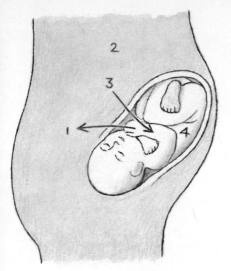

MOTHER IS RH NEGATIVE.
BABY IS RH POSITIVE.

1 Baby gives mother Rh factor.
2 Mother develops antibodies
   against Rh factor.
3 Mother gives baby anti-Rh antibodies.
4 Antibodies destroy
   baby's red blood cells.

The condition is even more serious when an unborn child has an Rh negative mother and an Rh positive father. The mother's blood may form an antibody against the child's Rh positive blood. It then can destroy the infant's red blood cells. But if the infant receives a large transfusion soon after it is born, its life can be saved. A new kind of vaccine, recently discovered, prevents the mother's system from attacking the red blood cells of her unborn child.

Even when an injury or disease does not cause a large loss of red blood cells, doctors may give a transfusion of plasma. The plasma builds up the volume of blood so that it can circulate freely. Blood plasma can be extracted easily from whole blood, and the red cells discarded. The yellowish plasma is allowed to stand for some time to be sure it is disease free. It can be stored, shipped, and used to save lives when fresh whole blood, which cannot be stored for long, is not on hand.

Up until about 40 years ago one of the most dangerous diseases was pernicious anemia. In this disease the bone marrow produces large immature red blood cells and not enough mature, ready-to-work cells.

Doctors discovered in 1927 that when liver was fed to patients with pernicious anemia, they improved immediately and were soon back to normal health. Research finally showed that the important thing in liver was vitamin B_{12}. Later research showed that another vitamin, folic acid, was also important in the building of blood. These vitamins are so potent that a bit the size of a pinhead can set the bone marrow to making normal cells.

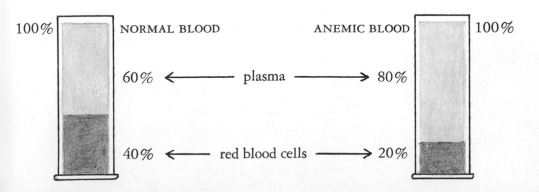

100%   NORMAL BLOOD   ANEMIC BLOOD   100%

60% ← plasma → 80%

40% ← red blood cells → 20%

Another job of the blood is to carry the hormone chemicals made by the ductless glands. Glands such as the pituitary, adrenal, thyroid, and the sex glands make hormone chemicals in small amounts. These chemicals are released into the blood regularly or as part of growth cycles. The blood, as a messenger, carries the hormones to all your tissues.

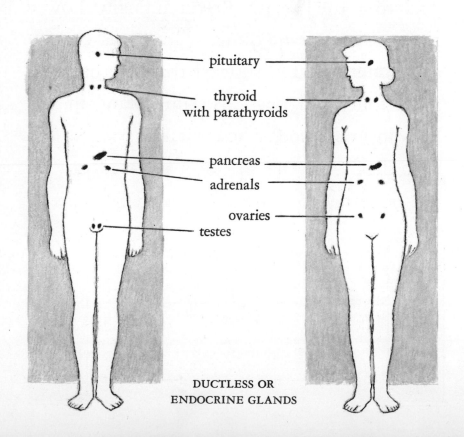

pituitary

thyroid
with parathyroids

pancreas

adrenals

ovaries

testes

**DUCTLESS OR
ENDOCRINE GLANDS**

PITUITARY HORMONES
Dwarfs have too little.
Giants have too much.

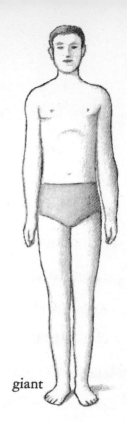

dwarf   normal   giant

Hormones are essential for normal growth. When they are lacking or in short supply, the growth pattern may be seriously disturbed. A lack of one pituitary hormone causes a type of dwarfism. If the pancreas gland fails to secrete the hormone insulin, the body has difficulty in using sugar and the disease diabetes results.

In addition to red blood cells your blood contains several kinds of white blood cells, or leucocytes. These cells are not white, but are nearly colorless. All have a nucleus, which red blood cells lose. But to see this nucleus and the other structures of a white blood cell, one must stain it with dyes.

Your blood contains fewer white blood cells than red—only about six to ten thousand in each cubic millimeter of blood—or one white blood cell to about every six hundred red blood cells.

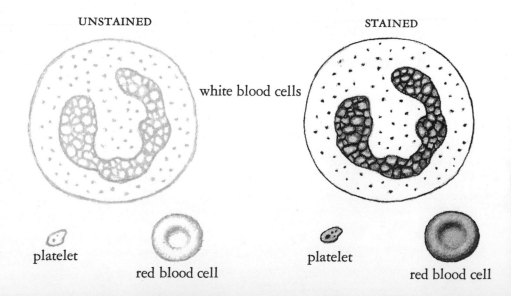

UNSTAINED

STAINED

white blood cells

platelet

red blood cell

platelet

red blood cell

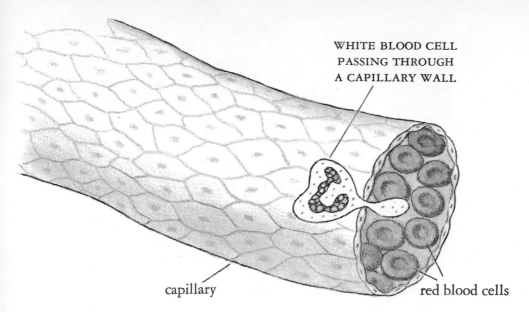

WHITE BLOOD CELL
PASSING THROUGH
A CAPILLARY WALL

capillary

red blood cells

White blood cells function somewhat like independent one-celled animals. Most of the time your blood flows in a network of tubes or blood vessels connecting your heart to all parts of your body. White blood cells can leave capillaries, the smallest blood vessels, and move into or around body tissues. They can change their shape and work their way through tiny spaces.

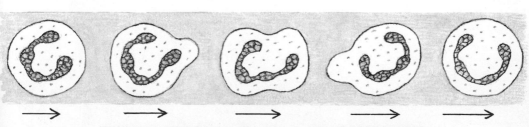

WHITE BLOOD CELLS CHANGE SHAPE AS THEY MOVE.

This ability to move around is essential to the job of white blood cells. They protect your body against invasion by bacteria or other parasites. Moving rapidly from blood vessels to a wound or infection, they surround bacteria and destroy them.

Once a bacteria is inside a white blood cell, enzyme chemicals digest it. At the same time some white blood cells may be destroyed by poisons from the bacteria. The remains of the bacteria, white cells, and fluids may form a

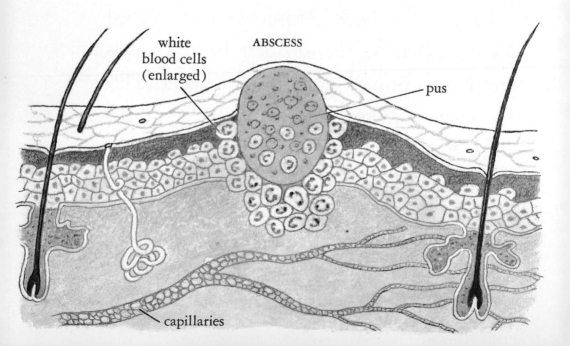

white
blood cells
(enlarged)

ABSCESS

pus

capillaries

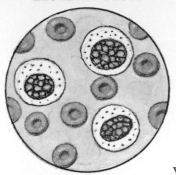

300,000	white blood cells (per cubic millimeter)	8000
many	immature white blood cells	none
few	red blood cells	normal

thick, yellowish material we call pus. A large pocket of pus is a boil, or an abscess. When one is located just under the skin it may break open, releasing the pus.

When an infection is severe your blood makes an increased number of white blood cells. If many white blood cells are destroyed, your body is less resistant to infections and diseases. Leukemia is a disease of the blood and blood-forming organs in which the number of white blood cells increases tremendously, and the number of red blood cells drops.

Six kinds of white blood cells are recognized by their origin, their size, and by the way they react to dyes. They differ in their functions. The larger white blood cells have a major role in destroying bacteria. The smaller white cells, lymphocytes, break down and form globulin, the chemical from which the blood makes antibodies. About half of a child's white blood cells are lymphocytes. In adults lymphocytes total about one third.

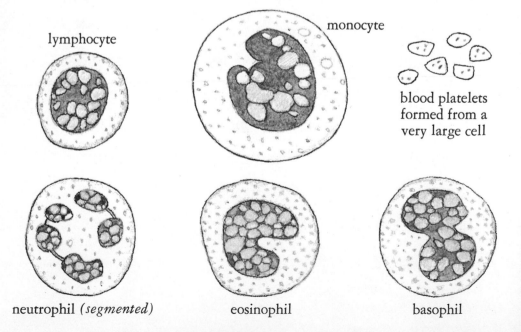

lymphocyte

monocyte

blood platelets formed from a very large cell

neutrophil (*segmented*)

eosinophil

basophil

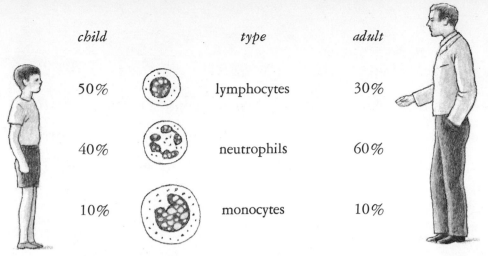

child		type	adult
50%		lymphocytes	30%
40%		neutrophils	60%
10%		monocytes	10%

CHANGES OF WHITE BLOOD CELLS WITH AGE

The last component of your blood is the many small fragments called platelets. They are not living cells. Each cubic millimeter of blood contains about 250 thousand platelets, which are important in clotting.

The liquid part of the blood, the plasma, is not completely confined to the blood vessels. As part of the blood it moves through the veins and arteries. But some of it leaves the small capillaries and flows through tissue spaces. There, as it bathes the body cells, it is called tissue fluid. Some plasma flows into other ducts, where it circulates in a different, but related system of lymph vessels. The blood liquid that circulates separately this way is called lymph.

There are some small changes as the plasma filters out and becomes lymph. Lymph normally contains no red blood cells and only the smallest white blood cells, the lymphocytes.

Lymph moves through fine vessels and through small spongy structures—lymph nodes —that help filter out the lymphocytes. When an infection is severe, lymph glands may swell. Equally important, the lymph absorbs digested fat from your intestines and passes it into the blood. When it nears the heart, lymph finds its way back into the bloodstream and again becomes part of the blood plasma.

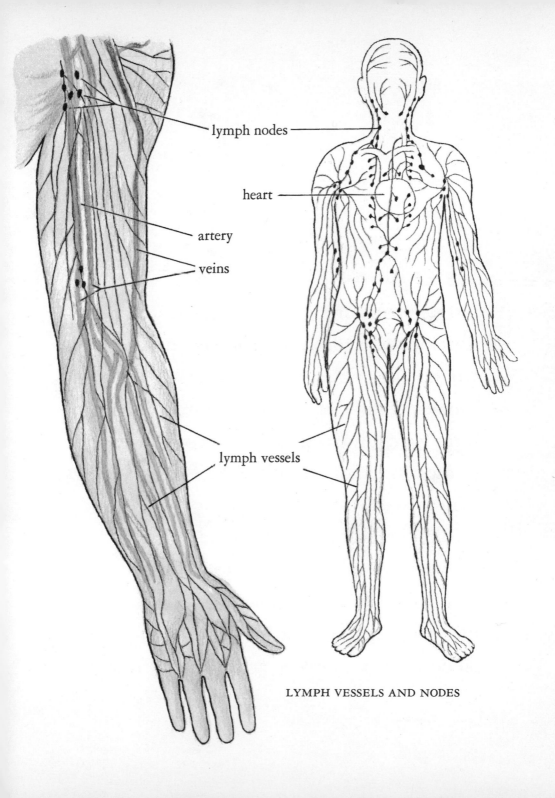

lymph nodes

heart

artery

veins

lymph vessels

LYMPH VESSELS AND NODES

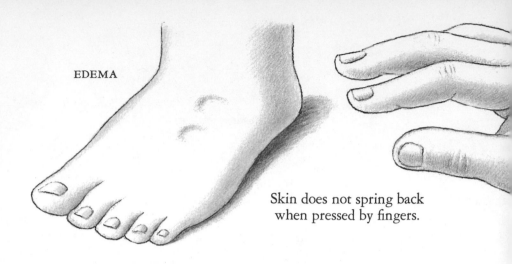

EDEMA

Skin does not spring back
when pressed by fingers.

In certain conditions or diseases, lymph does not move steadily but gathers in tissues, as around the ankles and below the eyes, giving people a puffy appearance. Lymph may also form welts under the skin of people who react to the protein of certain foods. These swellings are called hives.

Bleeding from a small wound or injury slows down and soon stops, because blood clots and seals the wound. Many blood chemicals that take part in clotting are present in the blood plasma. Others are released from the injured tissue of the wound and from blood platelets. The mixing of these chemicals forms threads of fibrin—a protein fiber. These fibers make a network that catches the red blood cells, slowing down and halting the flow of blood.

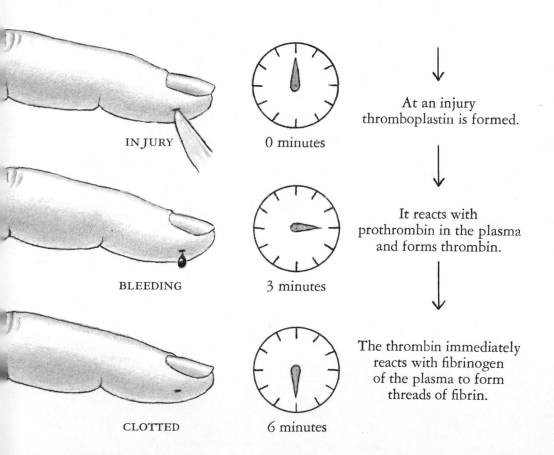

INJURY

0 minutes

At an injury thromboplastin is formed.

BLEEDING

3 minutes

It reacts with prothrombin in the plasma and forms thrombin.

CLOTTED

6 minutes

The thrombin immediately reacts with fibrinogen of the plasma to form threads of fibrin.

A few people inherit from their parents a condition in which their liver does not produce one of the chemicals essential for the clotting of blood. Such people are called bleeders and have hemophilia, the disease in which blood does not clot. Bleeders are normal people except that they must take great care not to get cut or injured, because their bleeding is hard to stop.

BLEEDERS AND CARRIERS OF HEMOPHILIA DESCENDED FROM QUEEN VICTORIA

Only men have the disease.

Queen Victoria — Prince Consort Albert

Duke of Albany — Princess Victoria-Eugenie — Princess Alice

Viscount Tromton — Prince Alphonso — Infante Gonzalo — Tsarevich Alexis

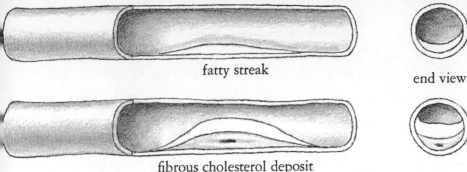

fatty streak

end view

fibrous cholesterol deposit

Much more serious are the problems caused when blood clots in places that should be free of obstruction. In these cases, the trouble is not usually in the blood itself but in the blood vessels.

As people grow older, deposits of fat or a limy material may form inside their blood vessels. This condition may be partly due to foods they eat and partly to the way they live. Such deposits are much more common in men than in women. At any rate, blood vessels become rough on the inside and blood flows more slowly. The heart pumps harder to keep the blood moving.

Sometimes a clot of blood forms at one of these rough spots. The clot may be carried through the blood vessel and lodge in some narrower place. Then the supply of blood is partly or completely cut off from the nearby tissues. These tissues quickly suffer from lack of food and oxygen that blood normally brings.

When a clot forms in the blood vessels around the heart, a person has coronary heart disease. When it happens in the blood vessels of the brain, a person has a stroke. Both are very serious and may cause death. As part of the treatment,

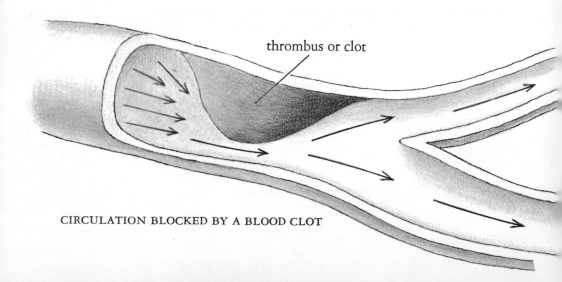

thrombus or clot

CIRCULATION BLOCKED BY A BLOOD CLOT

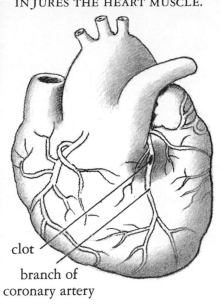

REDUCED OXYGEN SUPPLY
IN JURES THE HEART MUSCLE.

clot

branch of
coronary artery

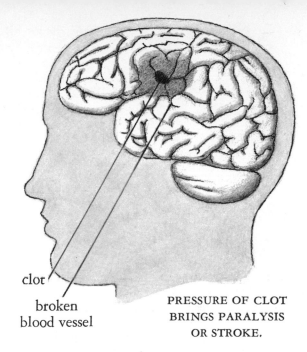

clot

broken
blood vessel

PRESSURE OF CLOT
BRINGS PARALYSIS
OR STROKE.

doctors sometimes give the patient chemicals that prevent clotting.

Bacteria, protozoa, and other disease organisms invade the blood. Some destroy red or white blood cells. Many produce poisons or toxins. These harmful toxins do not usually destroy the blood itself, but are carried by the blood to other parts of the body where damage is done. Diseases like yellow fever, typhoid, and sleeping sickness are examples.

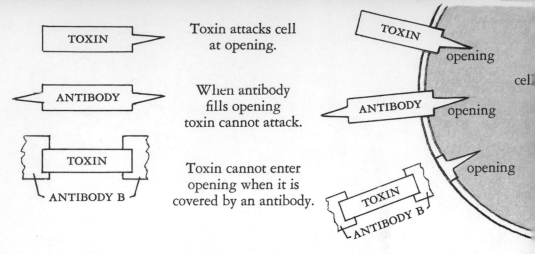

When disease occurs, the protein globulins of the plasma may form antibodies to combat or destroy the invader. The blood continues to make antibodies for a while, even after the disease has been checked. Thus extra antibodies remain in the blood. Should the same kind of invader enter the blood again, the antibodies that are already present will destroy the foreign organisms before the disease can get started. Each antibody that the blood produces reacts against a specific disease. Antibodies against diphtheria will not protect a child against smallpox or measles.

A great series of medical discoveries enable people to develop immunity and to build up antibodies without actually getting the disease. If weakened bacteria or viruses are injected into a person, his blood reacts and produces antibodies. He may become slightly ill, with a bit of fever, but the antibodies build up to a surplus that will keep him immune, or protected—often for years. This process is vaccination. Vaccinations for smallpox and polio are the best known ones.

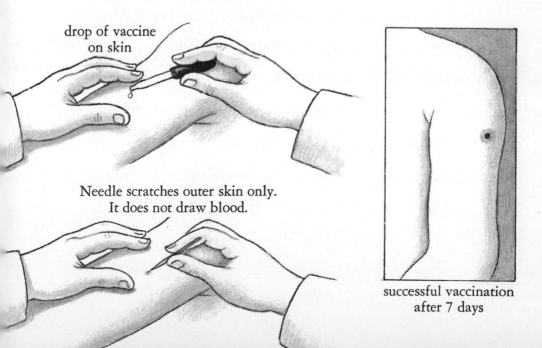

drop of vaccine on skin

Needle scratches outer skin only. It does not draw blood.

successful vaccination after 7 days

SERUM FROM
BLOOD OF AN
IMMUNIZED HORSE
PROTECTS US
AGAINST TETANUS.

A vaccinated person builds up antibodies in his own blood and so is actively protected. Another way to get the same effect is by injecting the bacteria or virus into a horse, or other large animal. Sometimes the material is injected into a growing chicken egg. Antibodies form, and a serum obtained from the blood can be injected into people to give them immunity—to typhoid, tetanus, and other diseases. Antitoxins, as they are called, also offer protection against the poisonous bites of snakes, scorpions, and spiders.

DISEASE		CAUSE	PREVENTED BY	LENGTH OF IMMUNITY
cholera		bacteria	vaccine	6 months to life
diphtheria		bacteria	toxoid	2 to 5 years
measles		virus	immune globulin	less than 6 months
mumps		virus	immune globulin	less than 6 months
plague		bacteria	vaccine	1 year
poliomyelitis		virus	oral vaccine	2 to 5 years
rabies		virus	vaccine	6 months to 1 year
scarlet fever		bacteria	vaccine	12 years
smallpox		virus	vaccine	5 to 7 years
tetanus		bacteria	toxoid	2 to 5 years
typhoid fever		bacteria	vaccine	5 to 8 years
typhus		rickettsia	vaccine	life
yellow fever		virus	vaccine	6 months to life

Plasma also has the job of distributing food and water all through your body. Within a few hours after a meal is eaten, the food is digested. It changes into liquids, which dissolve in or are carried by the blood plasma. Sugars, starches, fats, and proteins are changed during digestion in the stomach and intestines. They are reduced to simpler chemicals, which pass through digestive membranes into the lymph and blood systems. All these liquid food chemicals are then moved to the billions of living cells that use them to keep alive, to grow, and to function.

		where digested	*where absorbed*	*final state*
meat	PROTEIN	stomach	small intestine	amino acids
	FAT	first part of intestine	small intestine	triglycerides and fatty acids
bread	CARBOHYDRATE	stomach	small intestine	glucose

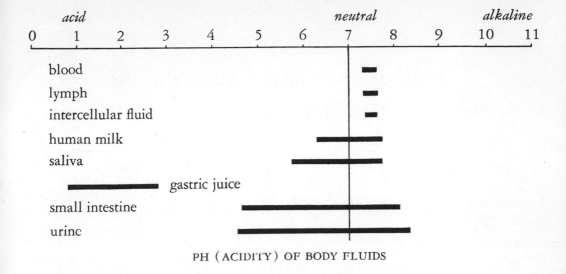

PH (ACIDITY) OF BODY FLUIDS

The vitamins and minerals in food are absorbed directly and do not need to be digested. Scores of minerals become dissolved in the blood plasma. Some are essential to the growth of bone. Others enable nerves to transmit messages. Your blood maintains a delicate balance of these minerals. For example, its chemical condition never becomes acid despite what TV commercials may say. These dissolved minerals (especially sodium and chlorine) make the blood something like seawater.

While doing its many tasks in the body, the blood itself is constantly changing. Most of these changes are normal and are part of your adjustment and growth. Some, however, are directly related to the state of your health. In

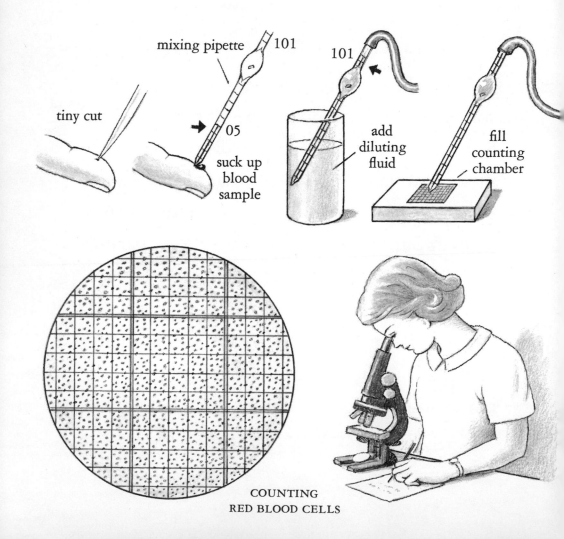

mixing pipette 101

101

tiny cut

05

suck up blood sample

add diluting fluid

fill counting chamber

COUNTING
RED BLOOD CELLS

case of illness (and often as a part of a routine health examination), your doctor takes a blood sample, which is sent to the laboratory. There a trained technician counts the red and white cells and performs tests that the doctor thinks necessary. The findings help him diagnose your illness or give a more complete picture of your health.

Because blood is so important, many people associate it with life itself. Blood has played a part in religion, including the Hebrew and Christian. Among the Aztec and other Indians of Middle America, worshipers made personal sacrifices to the gods by piercing their ear, tongue, or fingers with a sharp thorn. The Aztec believed that the sun-god lived on blood. As their nation grew, more and more prisoners were sacrificed to supply blood for this great deity.

AZTECS MAKING A BLOOD SACRIFICE

Sometimes a thousand prisoners were killed at feasts to give the sun-god the human blood he needed.

In parts of Asia a man and a woman made small cuts and used to mix their blood as part of their marriage vows. Blood was often used in ceremonies where people were adopted into

a tribe or when boys were initiated into man-
hood. A Watusi warrior of East Africa may
make a blood brother of a friend, even if he
is from another tribe. Amid feasting, each
makes a small cut near his navel and lets the
blood intermix. From then on the men are
pledged to lifelong friendship and mutual aid.

WATUSI WARRIORS' BLOOD BROTHERHOOD CEREMONY

Blood, though a liquid, is not very different from the other tissues of the body. That it is used as food, therefore, is not surprising. Many small animals feed on the blood of larger warm-blooded animals. Mosquitoes, lice, ticks, fleas, biting flies, midges, and leeches are some.

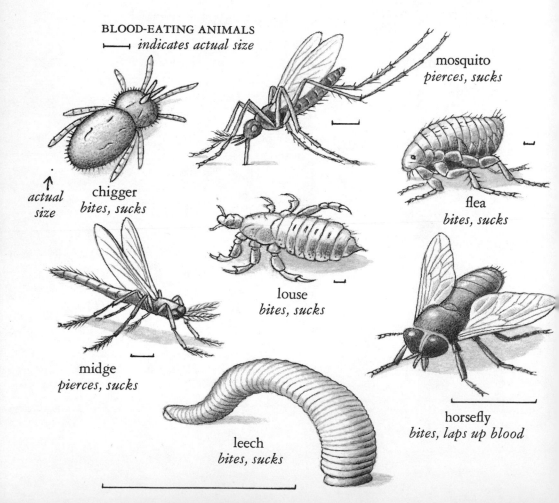

BLOOD-EATING ANIMALS
⊢——⊣ *indicates actual size*

mosquito
pierces, sucks

actual size

chigger
bites, sucks

flea
bites, sucks

louse
bites, sucks

midge
pierces, sucks

horsefly
bites, laps up blood

leech
bites, sucks

A special case is the vampire bat of Central and South America. This bat attacks cattle, other large animals, and even people, when they are asleep. With its rasping front teeth it gently scrapes the skin till the blood oozes out. The vampire laps up the blood as food, but does not consume enough to do much harm. Vampire bats are more feared because, in taking blood, they may transmit rabies or some other serious disease from one animal to another—and even to man.

Long ago people in southern Europe believed that the vampire was the soul of a dead person. It supposedly left the body at night to seek out victims and suck their blood. If the grave of a vampire was opened, so the stories said, the body would appear fresh and lifelike from its bloody meals, even though the person had been dead a long time. Such beliefs still exist in a few parts of the world.

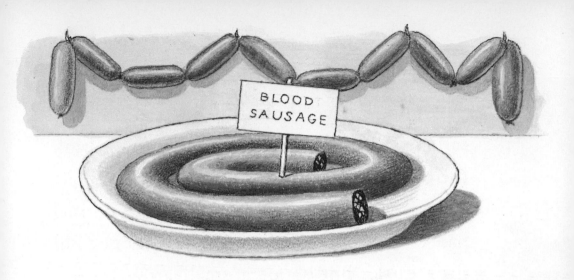

Much less gruesome than the story of the vampire is the fact that some people today find blood is an excellent food and use it constantly. When cattle are slaughtered for meat, the blood is saved to make into blood sausage or blood pudding. These two foods are common in parts of Europe and North America. Some groups of people (including ourselves) drain the blood from animals that are butchered. We prefer meat with little blood in it and think it tastes better. When stored, meat with only a little blood in it will keep better.

Among many hunting tribes, especially in earlier times, people gathered around to drink the blood whenever an animal was killed. Several tribes in Africa still use blood as a normal part of their diet. These cattlemen do not kill their cattle, but shoot a small arrow into a blood vessel. They collect the blood in a jar, and when they have taken a sufficient amount, without seriously harming the animal, they bind up the wound so that it can recover. Everyone takes the blood as food, especially the warriors.

We have an old saying that blood is thicker than water. So it is. But your blood began billions of years ago as the water of ancient seas. Now, thicker and much more complex, blood enables man to live, prosper, and to control an entire planet and the space around it.

MASAI GATHERING BULL'S BLOOD

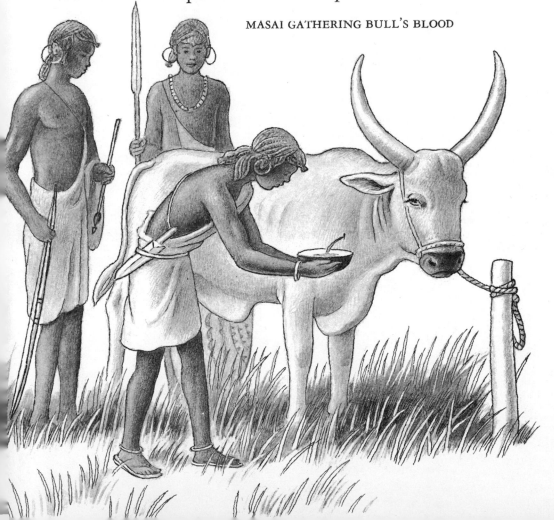

INDEX

Indicates illustrations